what not to wear

what not to wear

Trinny Woodall & Susannah Constantine

Photography by Robin Matthews

RIVERHEAD BOOKS
NEW YORK

To Sten and Johnnie with our Love always.

Riverhead Books
Published by The Berkley Publishing Group
A division of Penguin Group (USA) Inc.
375 Hudson Street
New York, New York 10014

Copyright © 2002 by Trinny Woodall and Susannah Constantine
Design and layout copyright © 2002 Weidenfeld & Nicolson
Cover design copyright © Claire Vaccaro

Previously published in the UK by Weidenfeld & Nicolson, 2002,
by arrangement with the BBC.
First Riverhead trade paperback edition: July 2003
Riverhead trade paperback ISBN: 1-57322-357-3

This book has been catalogued with The Library of Congress

Printed in the United States of America
10 9 8 7 6 5 4 3 2 1

what not to wear

contents

Looking stylish is as much about knowing **what not to wear** as it is about knowing what suits you. It's about **being honest** and coming to terms with the fact that **some parts of your body aren't great** and understanding that certain clothing only serves to exacerbate these problem areas. So many of us trundle through life not making the most of ourselves because **we are lacking in self-confidence**, convinced that clothes don't matter or have no idea where to begin. But the more you know about your body, the easier it is to look great.

Unfortunately, for a lot of us there are many hurdles to jump before we reach that stage and **we incorrectly believe the notion of becoming stylish is a feat way beyond our grasp**. We roll our inexperience in comforting excuses — there's the kids, the overdraft, no time, nor inclination. Clothes are immaterial, because you can rely on your fabulous personality and your partner is blind to you looking like a tramp, because he loves you just the way you are. At the end of the day this is bollocks. We believe there isn't a single one of you who doesn't want to **improve the way you look**. Even if you assume you have the style of a goddess, you'd probably like to trade in your boobs for a pair that defy gravity, and if you've got the boobs, you'd no doubt consider your butt too large to even contemplate displaying its cheeks in a tight pair of trousers.

You believe diet, money and surgery are the answers but you're too greedy to do the first, will never make the second and therefore can't pay for the third. If you can, however, accomplish all these, fantastic, but then of course your next apology is supposing you have to be fashionable to be stylish and if you are too old, too young, too thin, fat, tall or short it's not possible. **But looking stylish is not about following fashion**, losing weight, being rich or succumbing to the knife. **It's about dressing to show off what you love and hiding what you loathe about your body**. Once you really understand **what not to wear** the path to chic-dom becomes a piece of cake.

American fashion guru Diana Vreeland said "Elegance is innate...it has nothing to do with being well dressed." **The myth that you are born with style is incorrect** and an unfair supposition to bandy about. In our opinion it is actually codswallop. Would she be saying that about a born "elegantsia" dressed in an oversized fleece and leggings so tight they showed her cellulite? Would she say it to toothpick-thin fashion icon (and some say Ms. Vreeland's successor) Anna Wintour if she was wearing a plunging neckline that exposed her skeletal chest and a gathered skirt that swamped her oddly thin frame? We don't think so. You might have the grace of a prima ballerina, but if you have fat, pitted thighs no miniskirt, however gorgeous, is going to flatter them. **Style isn't something you are born with, but something any one of you can learn**.

We are prime examples of this. Should anyone think we do indeed have a modicum of style or lean toward possessing a good figure, they need to know that the former has taken years to accomplish and the latter is a complete deception. Our figures are tall and, in Trinny's case, thin, but any semblance of "nice bod" **boils down to clever disguise**. Trinny has always been passionate about clothes, devouring glossy mags from a tender age, but it took a good two decades to rid her of her theatrical passion for filching the look of the latest pop group. In the eighties, she owed a great deal to Spandau Ballet for her girl-meets-gay-boy, pinstripe suiting, while it was Bucks Fizz that paved the way for a fluffed and frosted barnet that was often capped by a jaunty trilby. Big earrings went with the big hair, both of which were set off by an orange skin tone courtesy of No.7 fake tan and pearly pink lipstick. This sounds vile and indeed it was, but her figure was always spoken of in the revered tones reserved for the extraordinary. The **truth as you will see is very different**. Trinny is thin, but thin with very short legs, no boobs and a disproportionately large and succulent butt. But because she has **learned to disguise**

these defects all the onlooker sees are endlessly long limbs and a sculpted arse, and because she dresses so well for her shape you don't even notice she's as flat as a prairie.

First impressions of Susannah may not be as favorable as Trinny, but some could think **oooh...sexy, curvy figure**. What a joke. Behind the neat-waisted jackets and three-quarter-length sleeves lies a body that is out of control and, after two kids, stretched beyond redemption. Her stomach needs stapling, her underarms hang as dramatically as the Gardens of Babylon and her boobs are way too large for human handling. Nevertheless, she has been **educated well in the art of camouflage**, but her style education didn't begin till she met Trinny, in spite of having worked with some of the world's leading designers. Susannah was schizophrenic in her lack of dress sense. It was vestal virgin meets King's Cross crack-crazed hooker. On the one hand she embraced all that was ghastly about Sloane Ranger dressing, while allowing her alterego to indulge in Marabou-trimmed gloves, laddered tights and unfeasibly teeny skirts. Someone once told her she had good legs, so one was lucky to ever catch her out of a skirt. The hair was extremely long with a swamping fringe aboard a short, fat neck that was forever throttled by a pearl choker. There was no discretion in her clothing but she got away with much of it **because the clothes suited her shape**.

Since those years of darkness we have worked in and seen the fashion industry from all angles. We regard "fashion" as a pretty frivolous affair, and the higher it gets, the more absurd it becomes. Yet when it comes to clothes it turns into something deadly serious. **When we shop we want our purchases to change our lives**. When we get dressed we want the Good Fairy to turn us into Elle Macpherson. Sadly, for most of us the Good Fairy is a manifestation born from nubile models posing from the gleaming pages of fashion magazines. These present unobtainable images that none of us mortals can even aspire to. The result of trying to look like them is one of immense frustration. You attempt to do it, but are often disappointed by the outcome. The frustration becomes all encompassing.

Having worked with an array of women for our television show *What Not to Wear* we have witnessed the female species' insecurity and frustration firsthand. Some of them thought clothes were ridiculous, others were sure they were beyond help. Many of the women could only see what they hated about their bodies. Once we pointed out that they had fabulous ankles, great boobs or a beautifully honed back **they felt**

encouraged that becoming stylish was possible. Many people may think our tactics harsh and unforgiving, but we are proud of the results. Every lady on our show has turned into **a gleaming example of confidence**.

Men think women are mad for getting so uptight about clothes. But we know that at the end of the day **the way we look can influence so much in our lives**. Looking sexy makes us feel sexy. Looking professional helps us get that job. **First, however, you need to get the shapes right.**

We hope that every woman who reads this book feels we are there bullying her into submission. Pass it on to your girlfriends, but keep it hidden from the boys and girls you don't like. The men don't need to know how **you have suddenly become a siren**. The competitive workmates can be kept in the dark as to why you look thinner, sleeker and more sophisticated. **This is your secret weapon, and remember, it's not so much about the tips you've been given, but more about the mistakes you have stopped making**. As long as you stick to the rules, you can forget what's in fashion. If, however, you have a passion for what's in fashion then **simply adapt this season's hot trend to your individual shape.**

People may look at you and think you have an amazing pair of boobs – **so what's the problem?** Well, for a start, Susannah knows, and Trinny can imagine, that buying dresses, suits and coats to fit both the top and bottom halves of your body requires a degree in anatomy. And while we're all in favor of a girl **making the most of her natural assets**, she needs to be careful not to look top-heavy or tarty. It is lovely having men magnets when you're out on the town, but there are times when you want to be appreciated for your brain power. This requires **decorous dressing** and the implementation of **surreptitious tricks** to tone things down. The primary tool, and one that will become indispensable, is a well-fitting bra. Invest whatever it takes to find the best one for you. Hoick them up high and push them forward with under-wires and strong straps. Armed with **the right bra**, you are in control of your jugs rather than the other way around. It's much more exciting having breasts that can be exhibited as and when the occasion requires.

big boobs

1

**high neck
and
sleeveless**

why: makes boobs
look like balloons
semi-filled with
water.

worst t-shirt

<u>or</u>
high round-neck t-shirts
why: molds boobs into one big lump.

wide-open neckline

why: a low, wide neckline breaks up the chest and prevents your boobs from looking like they are an extension of your chin.

alternative
V-neck sleeveless t-shirts

why: the V breaks up the expanse of your chest (no sleeves are for that rare bird blessed with toned arms and a pert chest).

unfitted, sleeveless shell top

why: breasts take on a lumpy quality like badly made custard.

worst top

or
round-neck tanks

why: large breasts invariably have big arms to carry them and these should remain hidden at all times.

tight around the waist and loosening on breasts

why: because the fabric is looser on the chest it gives the illusion of not having too much to fill it. Your waist will also look tiny by comparison.

corset shape with sleeves

why: accentuates breasts without being vulgar.

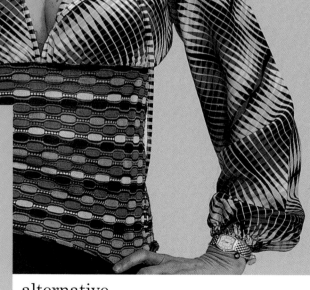

alternative
wrap tops

why: pull breasts forward and spotlight waist.

boxy, short-waisted jacket

why: makes you look square, shapeless and top-heavy.

<u>or</u>

princess collar

why: anything buttoned at the neck will give you larger boobs than you need.

very fitted, deep V, with hem cut to hip and a small lapel

why: short length lengthens legs and deep V divides the chest.

best jacket

halterneck

why: hard to wear a bra, which means boobs creep out at the sides.

worst dress

or
spaghetti-strap slip
why: thinness of straps enhances size of shoulders and breasts.

wrap dress

why: pulls in the waist and divides and separates the bust

sweetheart neckline, empire line and three-quarter-length sleeves

why: makes the neck long and elegant, rather than bunching boobs up to the chin.

alternative

cocktail dress with low draw-string neckline

why: hides tummy; gathered fabric helps to dwarf size of chest and prevents boob-clinging.

chunky knit
why: thick wool equals thick torso.

or
polo necks
why: boobs take on a new role as third chin.

alternative
**round-neck cardigan
undone to the top of your bra**

why: shows off that stunning cleavage – with the added bonus of being able to do it up when cold or feeling overexposed.

alternative
deep V neck in a fine knit

why: fine cashmere will keep you warm and looking svelte, while the deep V will divide the breasts, showing your God-given two, as opposed to an odd one.

wrap cardigan

why: you can make it as tight as you wish with the boobs always being kept apart.

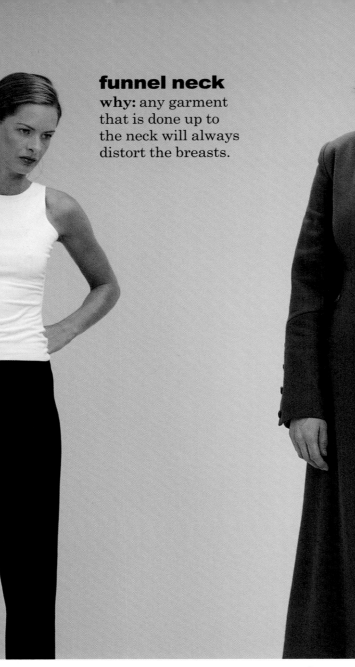

funnel neck

why: any garment that is done up to the neck will always distort the breasts.

<u>or</u>
double-breasted anything
why: two rows of buttons broaden the chest – not good for creating a body of perfect proportions.

<u>and</u>
belted trench
why: creates an uncalled-for billowing around an already breasty area.

**tight waist
with narrow
lapel and
full skirt**

why: the depth of
neckline breaks up
the expanse of
swollen flesh.

	no guilt	slight guilt	guilt for days
t-shirt	Gap H & M Target	Juicy Couture Velvet	Chloé Helmut Lang Marc Jacobs
sweater	Club Monaco Zara J. Crew	Joseph French Connection Vanessa Bruno	TSE cashmere Ballantyne Malo
top	H & M Zara Express	Betsey Johnson Catherine Malandrino Diane von Furstenburg Vanessa Bruno	Missoni Tracy Feith Rozae Nichols Anna Molinari for Blumarine
coat	H & M Zara Club Monaco	Marc by Marc Jacobs See by Chloé Joseph Earl Jean	Dolce & Gabbana Dries Van Noten
dress	H & M Anthropologie Express	Betsey Johnson Ghost Joseph Diane von Furstenburg	Alberta Ferretti Chloé Diane von Furstenburg
jacket	Banana Republic H & M Gap	Paul & Joe Nanette Lepore Kors by Michael Kors	Michael Kors Dolce & Gabbana Veronique Branquinho

shopping

golden rules for for big boobs

Never wear high round necks.

Never wear cable knit sweaters.

Nehru jackets are for men only.

Don't ever leave the house without doing the bra test. If you can see the contours of padding or lace, take it off.

Avoid ribbed polo necks – they make your boobs look like they grow from your neck.

Chuck out the clothes that don't suit you – even if you think of them as old friends.

Never put on underwear that's darker than the clothes you're wearing.

golden rules

Subtle is sexy – vulgar is not

If you are the owner of **a chest bereft of boobs**, you have no doubt longed for them, thought about surgery and tried all breast-enhancing trickery to boost what isn't there. The ironic thing is, many buxom women look at the daintily endowed with envy. Susannah longs to be able to wear clothes that Trinny can. Loads of **clothes look better** worn by flat-chested women. They hang better and this must surely be a compensating factor for worrying about not being sexy. You **don't need knockers to be alluring** and at least you have the choice of a breast day or a non-breast day. You can boost your sexiness with padded bras and silicone extras. We know it's hard sometimes for the unattached, because young men especially need an eyeful of breast before they even talk to you. Maybe this isn't such a bad thing, as turn this notion on its head and **your dainty boobs** are actually a filter for all the jerks out there. **An added bonus** is that there isn't a single coat or jacket you won't look fab in.

no boobs

why: accentuates a
bony chest which
looks more like a
deflated balloon than
a swelling cleavage.

worst t-shirt

or

**deep V neck with three-quarter-length
sleeves**

why: the V acts as an arrow to the disappointment
of not having anything to fill it. Three-quarter-
length sleeves show the thinnest part of the wrist,
making the overall effect way too skeletal.

high neck tank with cut-away sleeves

why: attention is drawn to the arms, which are invariably slim.

best t-shirt

alternative
slash neck with capped sleeves

why: the slash broadens shoulders and the capped sleeves create coat hanger angles normally reserved for models.

corset

why: designed to enhance the chest, if there is nothing to bolster then the whole thing becomes redundant.

worst top

or
boob tube

why: on a girl with breasts it looks cool, on a girl with none it becomes a bandage with nothing to keep it in place.

halterneck

why: yes, there are bras designed to wear with these, but little breasts work in tandem with the angular cut of this top. They also show off a shoulder, which is a sexy substitute to a cleavage.

alternative
sleeveless top with detailed front panel
why: frills and froth cover the chest and make up for what is not there.

empire line

why: hangs like a habit on a nun from a very strict order. No need for a chastity belt here.

<u>or</u>
**skintight and stretchy
with spaghetti straps**
why: skintight on a skinny top half isn't sexy, it's a disappointment.

high neck and a little see-through

why: tiny breasts can get away with subtle nipple display. As long as it's not too overt it can be truly sexy.

plunging neckline down to navel

why: you can't do this look if you require artificial uplift, but it's fabulously seductive if you don't.

best dress

alternative
backless

why: a beautiful back is just as desirable as a heaving chest.

anything too fine and low

why: the gossamer fabric clings to the skin, creating a wet t-shirt effect, clutching raisins as opposed to peaches.

worst sweater

chunky polo neck

why: on a woman blessed with a flat chest these look immeasurably elegant — the roll neck looks like a roll neck, as opposed to an extra chin on a woman with boobs.

best sweater

alternative
fitted long sleeves with round neck

why: the simple lines of this shape are not ruined by the bulk of large bosoms.

shopping

	no guilt	slight guilt	guilt for days
t-shirt	H & M Club Monaco Petit Bateau	Juicy Couture Marc by Marc Jacobs	Chloé Marni Gucci
top	H & M Club Monaco Express	Theory Nicole Farhi Vanessa Bruno	Alice Temperley Chloé Prada Miu Miu Pucci
sweater	J. Crew Banana Republic Zara	Agnès b. Joseph John Smedley	Marni Prada Gucci Etro
dress	Zara H & M	Tocca A. B. S. Nicole Farhi Carmen Marc Valvo	Narcisco Rodriguez Tuleh Marc Jacobs

golden rules for no boobs

Plunging necklines are only for perfect décolleté undamaged by the sun or age.

Corsets are for those with boobs.

Flat chests need high necklines.

Chicken fillets for breast enhancement must always be secured with a bra or they will fall in the soup at dinner.

Backs are sexy alternatives, so keep them shiny and exfoliated.

Chuck out the clothes that don't suit you – even if you think of them as old friends.

If you're wearing a V-neck sweater, always wear a round-necked t-shirt underneath.

You might think a scoop neckline gives the appearance of breasts – but all it does is show off an empty space.

Remember, you may not have been born with style but you can create it

Big arms are the bane of this nation, not that the nation seems to give a damn. Women unashamedly baring huge arms **that need to be covered** continually confront us. We don't, however, lay the blame at their feet. It's the manufacturers who should be shot for not knowing their market. They are hell-bent on mass-producing tops and dresses with no sleeves and these in turn are the ones photographed for the magazines. Susannah, whose upper arms could feed a family of six, finds the **lack of sleeves depressing**. Flicking through the glossies each month, her heart breaks. What the hell is she, the owner of plucked chicken wings, **supposed to wear in the summer?** What in God's name should one do for an evening frock if the arms need covering? Go to the ball looking like a dowager duchess or just not bother? If there were more sleeves around, the problem of naked jiggling flesh would cease to exist and women like Susannah would **no longer feel the frustration of having to make do** with t-shirts, cardigans and dowdy dresses.

cap sleeves

why: on big arms these look like a stretched swimming cap atop a mountain of flesh.

worst t-shirt

or
sleeveless tank

why: do you really want the world to see your most hideous physical defect? Hide the buggers, for goodness sake.

alternative
long-sleeve t-shirts
why: the sleeves obviously hide the sins; just be sure they aren't too tight and resemble vacuum-packed frankfurters.

three-quarter-length sleeves
why: to hide the flab at the top and display delicate wrists.

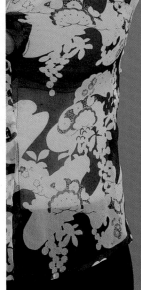

puff sleeves

why: elastic sleeves will create two very fat sausages, as opposed to one.

or

halterneck

why: the narrowness of the top at the neck will only spotlight the comparative hugeness of the arms.

floating cuffs

why: cuffs in a flimsy fabric add a certain delicacy to beefy arms while hiding the heftier truth.

alternative
puff at shoulder seam

why: a roomier armhole fits a fatter arm and the blouson effect doesn't squeeze, which gives the impression of something altogether more elegant being inside.

spaghetti straps

why: the delicacy of these filigree strings only highlights the massiveness of your upper arms.

or

sleeveless shift dress

why: people will wonder how that gargantuan mass of flesh managed to squeeze through the armhole.

fluted sleeves – the more exaggerated the better

why: like a bootleg trouser on a heavy thigh, the breadth of the cuff balances out thick upper arms.

alternative
sleeves

why: on anything sleeves elongate the forearms, making the entire garment more elegant and willowy.

alternative
sleeved dress in a small pattern

why: the busyness of the pattern detracts from the arm.

big bangle

why: by rights this should make the arm look thinner. As you see it doesn't because it's hiding the thinnest part...your wrist.

worst jewelry

delicate
bracelet

why: shows off and prettily decorates the finest part of your arm.

	no guilt	slight guilt	guilt for days
t-shirt	Club Monaco Gap Zara Target	Velvet DKNY Three Dots	Giorgio Armani Helmut Lang
top	Express H & M Zara	Vanessa Bruno Catherine Malandrino Dosa	Missoni Chloé
dress	Anthropologie H & M Zara	Betsey Johnson Dosa Diane von Furstenburg	Dolce & Gabbana Giorgio Armani Donna Karan

golden rules for big arms

Fat arms must always wear sleeves.

Capped sleeves are an absolute no – they strangle big arms.

Small prints cover a multitude of flabby flesh.

Be ruthless – chuck out the clothes that don't suit you and treat yourself to some new ones that do.

Don't be scared of appearing different from your friends

golden rules

3

Most big butt bearers hate their rumps. But as long as it's pert **it doesn't matter how huge it is**. There is something very sexy about a rounded rear, so rather than trying to hide it, **show it off**. Don't be frightened to wear tight skirts; a man would far rather have something meaty to cling on to. In dressing a butt, think about how a pregnant tummy looks best.

One that is shown off by **tight clothing** is much more flattering than one that is tented by swathes of fabric. Material that hangs too voluminously from the fleshiest part of a protruding butt makes your thighs and arse mould into one mass.

A bum that is disproportionately vast isn't great, so **the sly use of tricks** to deceive the eye into believing it's more in proportion is what you need.

The bummer about **fleshy buns** is that if a skirt or pair of trousers fits around the arse, it may well not fit your waist.

It might just be then that you have to resign yourself to the local seamstress who can take in the loose fabric.

high-waisted and tight

why: waistband cut high around the waist makes butt look bigger because there is more fabric.

or
front pleats

why: pleats will be pulled out by fat backside.

and
tapered trousers

why: make your ankles slim, but Jesus, does your arse look enormous above them.

side-fastening, loose-fitting trousers

why: the lower waist-band cuts the butt area in half making it in turn half the size.

alternative
wide-leg trousers

why: keep it all well balanced, as they don't so much cup the butt as hang softly away from it.

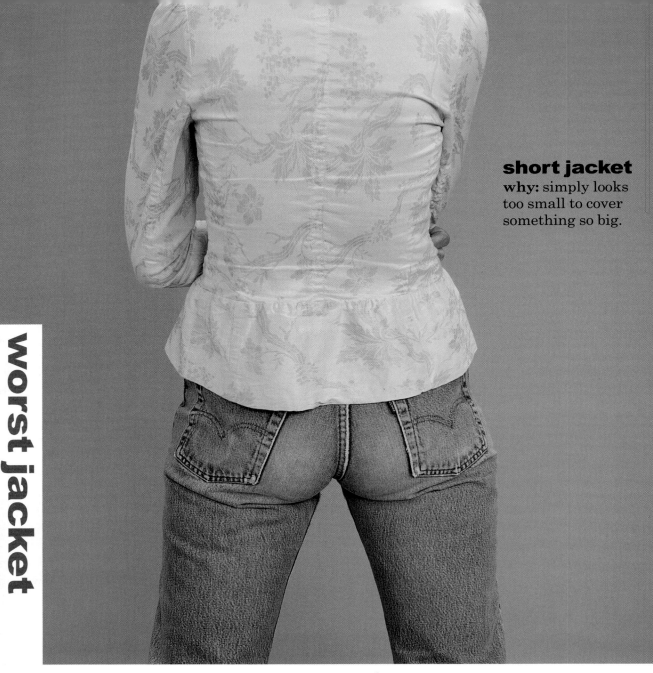

short jacket
why: simply looks too small to cover something so big.

worst jacket

or
jackets ending on or above your backside
why: will only exaggerate its width.

and
long, straight coat with no definition
why: will be too tight around the butt and too loose on the waist.

alternative
slimline jacket that ends under butt
why: covers bodily sin while keeping a sharp
silhouette and whitewashing the truth.

best jacket

**a tailored look
that flares
over the butt**
why: hides and
balances the butt,
giving a feminine shape.

A-line

why: a big butt in an A-line skirt balloons the fabric out at the back, making it enormous in comparison with legs. Looks like a pregnant tummy in reverse.

<u>or</u>

straight skirt

why: hangs unattractively from arse making your thighs look wide and calves like little pins emerging from the Lincoln Tunnel.

flared

why: clasps the butt and kicks out from the back of the thighs giving an S-shaped elegance to your rounded buttocks.

a pencil skirt

why: clings in all the right places and made up in a tailored fabric has a corset effect that keeps it all together.

best skirt

large prints in a soft fabric

why: floaty fabric offers no help in terms of holding the flab in and a bold print will only make a mountain range out of an outsized molehill.

or
long dresses cut on the bias
why: will make your butt look like a lollipop on a stick.

and
rear-squeezing dresses
why: if it's a close fit on your butt, it won't fit anywhere else.

**tailored or
fitted dress
(but please,
no shifts)**

why: gives a
controlled, yet sexily
displayed outline.

	no guilt	**slight guilt**	**guilt for days**
trousers	Zara	French Connection	Giorgio Armani
	J. Crew	Agnès b.	Alice Temperley
	Club Monaco	Laundry	Comme des Garçons
	Nuala by Puma		
jacket/coat	Banana Republic	Joseph	Alice Temperley
	H & M	Theory	Chloé
	Zara	Tommy Hilfiger	Costume National
			Alice and Olivia
skirt	Zara	French Connection	Prada
	H & M	Agnès b.	Dolce & Gabbana
	Banana Republic	Nanette Lepore	Dries Van Noten
		Kors by Michael Kors	
dress	Zara	Joseph	Anna Molinari
	Express	A. B. S.	Marc Jacobs
	Club Monaco	Diane von Furstenburg	Donna Karan
	H & M		

golden rules for big butts

Never wear jackets that end at the butt.

Any panty line on the rear is revolting.

Put on the outfit you feel most confident in and work out why you like it so much. What does it cover and what does it reveal?

Hipster trousers cut your butt in half.

High-waisted trousers make your butt look HUGE.

Friends may be rude about
your newfound style –
it's only because they are jealous

golden rules

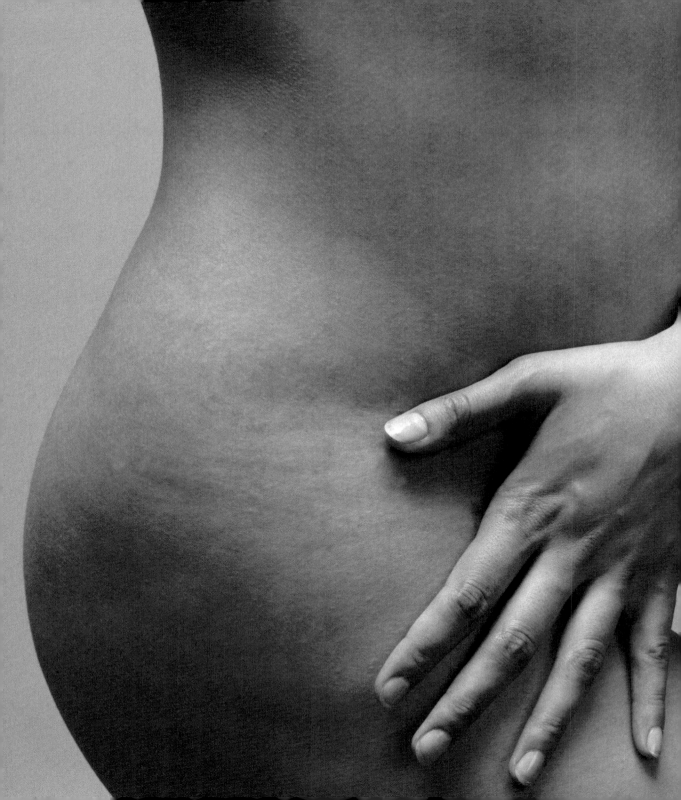

Not having a waist can **stifle a woman's femininity**. Just look at the lengths they went to in creating an almost obligatory 18-inch girth in the past. **Thickening middles** were winched in with necessary ferocity by corsets that regularly made the wearer pass out. And why? **To craft the classic female form**, which resembled an exaggerated hourglass — curvaceous and womanly in its shape, acceptable to society in its symbolism. Thankfully, we are way beyond those days of implementing strict distinctions between the sexes and now have the **freedom to be what the hell we want**. That said, it would be nice not to be mistaken for a bloke from the rear view. Corsets can do wonders for a girl's waist, but they aren't the only thing able to give what your genes chose not to.

no waist

5

baggy sacks

why: you may have as much form as a tower block, but that doesn't mean to say you have to enhance it with shapeless clothing.

or

boxy cardigans

why: square in cut, these ill-defined sins make a woman as sexy as a cardboard box. Or even less so.

navel-deep Vs

why: these slice up the slab of torso, making you less a woman of substance and more a being of refined beauty.

corset tops

why: there is nothing like a bit of boning to create that elusive hourglass body.

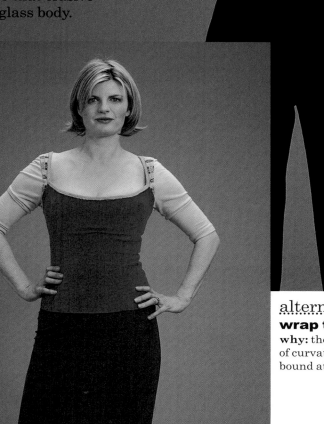

alternative
wrap tops

why: the wrapped fabric creates the illusion of curvature, particularly when the ties are bound at the side of the waist.

double-breasted

why: the two rows of straight-stitched buttons make no effort to convince the eye that there is indeed a waist under that jacket.

or
bolero jacket

why: these are so short that they leave your entire waist exposed to scrutiny and salacious comments.

alternative
short zip-front leather
why: worn with a belt slung just below, this will make the lower-waist bigger, thus minimizing the waist above.

best jacket

waisted within an inch of its life
why: a tailored waist will naturally flare out over the hips, cultivating curves where there are none.

the trench

why: undone, this is a pathetic excuse for a coat and will do nothing but swamp any semblance of femininity. Belted, it will draw attention to the stress the belt is under to meet around your middle.

or

straight-cut overcoat

why: if it fits your waist, it will bag over your backside.

best coat

frock coat

why: as these have a fabulous waist cut into them, don't ruin the curvaceous line by doing it up. Let the coat do the work for you.

worst dress

the shift

why: think back to the Princess of Wales's worst looks and they will surely be one of those ghastly shift dresses she wore. Not blessed with a waist, she looked very mannish in this most dull of dresses, that have only ever looked good on Jackie Onassis. The reason? She was fragile to the extreme, with great legs, no breasts and a very square jaw.

alternative
wrap dress

why: as with a wrap top, a wrap dress helps the art of deception.

fitted, made in soft material with small print

why: the busyness of the fabric draws attention away from the real story of not having a waist underneath it. Delicate fabric is an added distraction, as there is always some movement to it.

shopping

	no guilt	slight guilt	guilt for days
top	Zara H & M	Velvet DKNY	Tracy Feith Veronique Branquinho Missoni
coat	Club Monaco Zara H & M	Joseph Searle Agnès b.	Dolce & Gabbana Alexander McQueen Alice Temperley MaxMara
jacket	H & M Zara Express	Joseph Nanette Lepore Marc by Marc Jacobs	Vivienne Westwood MaxMara Dolce & Gabbana
dress	Express Anthropologie	Betsey Johnson Diane von Furstenburg	Vivienne Westwood John Galliano Ralph Lauren

golden rules for no waist

Never wear baggy sacks.

Deep V necks cinch in the waist.

The corset has become more comfortable since the 19th century, so invest in one.

Thick belts around the hips make the waist appear smaller.

Bandage underwear is like pastry under a rolling pin – it flattens it all out.

All things double-breasted must be chucked out.

Tailored coats left undone create the appearance of a waist.

Give your wardrobe a good workout – it's twice as satisfying as a day's shopping

golden rules

If you've got or don't want perfect boobs, then it will be **long legs** you're after. These, like lovely breasts, are a reason to hate anyone who owns them, especially as cosmetic surgery is yet to perfect a method of **increasing the inside leg measurement**. Trinny sympathizes wholly with stump owners. She's had them all her life. Rather than live with them, though, she has learned **how to hide them**, quite brilliantly. No one would guess that lurking beneath those **long-line jackets and fully flared trousers** are pins better attached to one of Snow White's small friends. If she can **give the illusion of legs** to rival Elle Macpherson, anyone can. And like all easily solved problems, it frustrates us immensely to see women who have given in to the fact that they are Corgis rather than Great Danes.

cropped

why: a trouser that ends anywhere above the anklebone is shortening. When people look at legs encased in short trousers, all they see is, well, the short trousers and this in turn makes short legs look even...shorter.

<u>or</u>
drainpipe jeans
why: far too tight leaving no room for manipulating the truth. Your short legs are left too exposed in these.

<u>and</u>
high-waisted trousers
why: these just visually increase the length of your back and highlight exactly how low-slung your arse really is.

palazzo pants

why: cover where your butt ends and your waist begins, thus making short legs appear longer.

best trousers

alternative
color coordination
why: wearing the same color trousers, socks and shoes will elongate the length of the legs.

alternative
wide flares
why: the width of the flare will cover any shoe no matter how high. Just be sure they are long enough in your chosen footwear to still skim the floor.

6

anything too tight

why: will clutch around the butt giving away the terrible secret of having a butt that almost drags along the floor.

worst dress

one worn over trousers

why: this is a great trick for disguising how short your legs really are because the trousers are shielded by extra coverage in the form of the dress.

long and high-waisted

why: like anything empire line, the dress flares from under the bust, glancing over the bum and therefore wiping it out completely.

best dress

6

short and alone

why: these leave a gap at the stomach, which equates to not having long enough legs to rise up and meet the hem of the top.

worst top

two tops layered

why: if you have short legs, you'll have a long back to compensate for the stuntedness. Your expanse of torso needs to be broken up with layering, which will automatically make your legs look longer.

best top

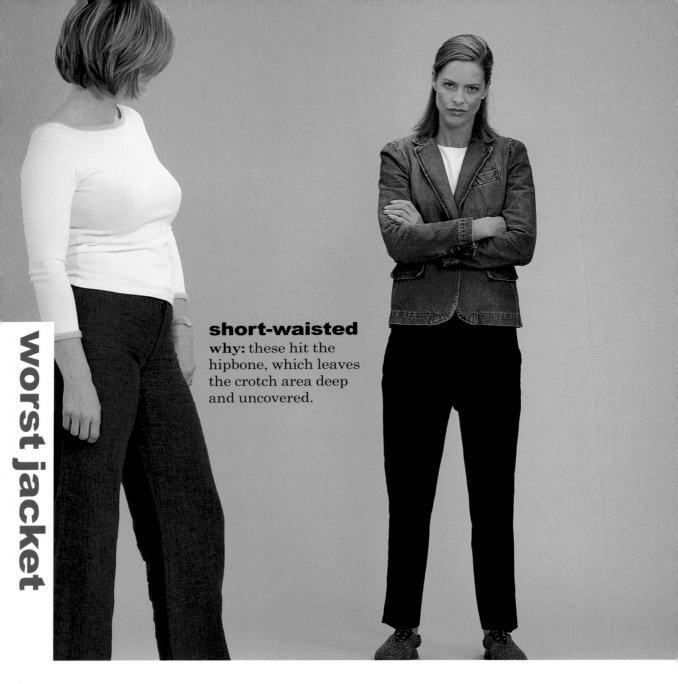

short-waisted

why: these hit the hipbone, which leaves the crotch area deep and uncovered.

three-quarter length

why: this is a great length as long as it is worn with trousers and heels, otherwise it will swamp you.

alternative
long-line

why: these are the ones that end just under the butt and show as much of the legs as possible.

bias cut ending mid-calf

why: this difficult length doesn't show enough leg to elongate it and too much to hide the fact that legs aren't your strong point.

or
long skirt and flat shoes

why: this will make you look like a long-legged person...whose pins have been chopped at the knee.

long with high heels

why: as long as the shoes are covered all will assume it's your legs rather than the shoes that are giving you extra height.

calf length with high boots

why: wear these in the same color and people will focus on your high butt perched at the top of endless legs.

best skirt

alternative
ending just below knee
why: not only is this the thinnest part of your leg, but it leaves your entire calf open to the public, thus giving it the opportunity to show its maximum length.

	no guilt	slight guilt	guilt for days
trousers	Zara	Katayone Adeli	Chloé
	J. Crew	Theory	Commes des Garçons
	Express	7 for all Mankind	Tuleh
dress	Zara	Joseph	Marni
	Banana Republic	BCBG	Tuleh
	J. Crew		
top	J. Crew	APC	Prada
	Club Monaco	DKNY	Chloé
	Zara	Nicole Farhi	Alice Temperley
		Jigsaw	Stella McCartney
jacket/coat	H & M	Laundry	Marni
	Zara	Agnès b.	MaxMara
		Theory	Costume National
skirt	H & M	French Connection	Plein Sud
	Anthropologie	Agnès b.	Dries Van Noten
		Cynthia Rowley	Ralph Lauren

golden rules for short legs

Cropped trousers will only accentuate your lack of leg.

Never wear tight trousers – they will only draw attention to where your butt ends and your legs begin.

Always wear your hem to the ground when wearing trousers with high heels.

Never wear a skirt that has a second dropped waistband – your already short legs will halve again in size.

Dresses over trousers cover up where the legs begin.

Keep the color flowing – same on shoe, sock and trouser.

If you can't walk in your high heels, they won't give you confidence.

Hang colored clothes together as outfits – so you always have something to wear

golden rules

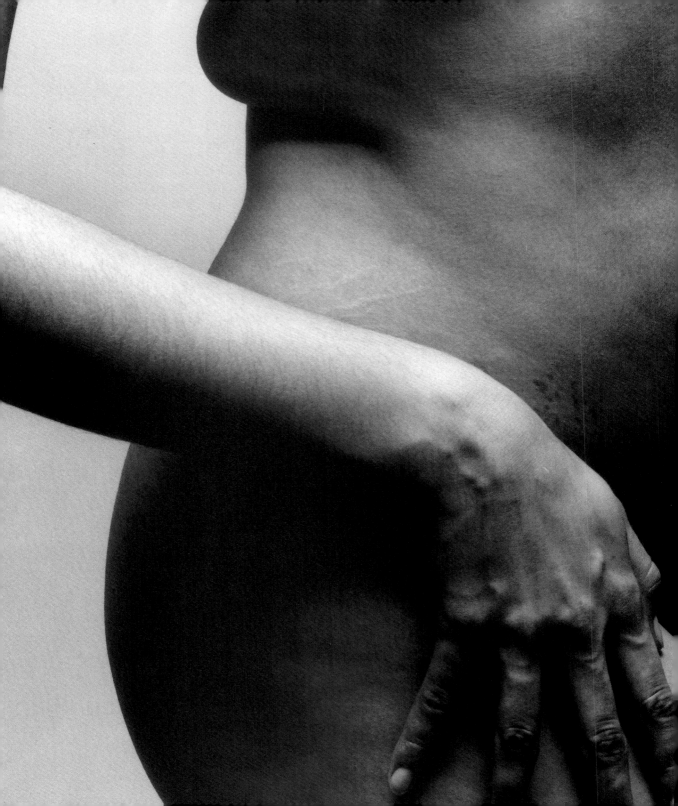

Joint winner with pear-shape as the **least favored body part** is the stomach. There are few women who are the proud owners of a toned tummy and those that are are either genetic freaks or work out relentlessly to achieve concrete control. The rest remain **burdened by flab** that has a life of its own. It's a ghastly affliction, this whole tummy thing, because the goal of any exercise program is a six-pack. We're driven to believe that it's not possible to have a beautiful body with **fat hanging over your waistband**. This is terrible for any of us who have so much as looked at a doughnut or even thought about babies, let alone heaved one of them out. We understand that childbirth, like a normal, healthy appetite can do terrible things to the body, but without surgery it's damn near impossible to firm up skin that has been stretched beyond redemption. So, **if you can't beat it, conceal it**.

skin-clinging

why: there is nothing worse than a too-tight bra strap being shown slicing through excess fatty tissue in a spray-on t-shirt. Added to this, a front view of rippling flab dribbling down one's side is enough to make Samson want to remain blind.

or
short t-shirt

why: t-shirts that end an inch or two above your waistband allow the largest roll to burst through.

shirt-tail hem

why: these scoop down and gently cover the tummy at the front, while lifting at the side to reveal a hopefully slimmer hip bone.

alternative
slim-fit

why: as long as it doesn't claw at the fat a skinny-fit t-shirt fines a bulky torso down, because you look neat and therefore trim.

alternative
mid-length tops

why: a hem that stops in the middle of the tummy visually breaks up the bulge.

alternative
tight over breasts

why: a snug fit around the breasts will mean looser fabric on tummy, allowing the boobs to take center stage.

worst top

tight tank

why: these always ride
up over the rolls to reveal
a pillow of flab hanging
over your waistband.

ruched top

why: no one will know if it is the fabric or your flesh that is making the waves.

alternative
wrap top

why: the ties are unusually high enough to winch in the waist, leaving the skirt of the top to swathe over the tummy.

spray-on lycra

why: you look like too much meat stuffed into a sausage skin.

worst dress

or
kaftan

why: if you are large anywhere these make everything else look even more enormous.

alternative
wrap dress

why: exaggerate the folds and you camouflage the tummy.

alternative
empire line

why: the focus is on the breasts with the fabric falling from just beneath them. This acts as a tent without hiding your entire figure.

low-slung waist

why: this will cling around the hips, acting as good a cover-up as a wide belt over your tummy.

gathered waist

why: why do you want a bulky skirt – isn't a bulging stomach enough?

or

straight-cut skirt

why: the skirt will hang from the continental shelf of flab making your entire pelvic area look huge.

alternative

sarong skirt for the more mature or sarong for the younger woman

why: movement of folds hides the motion going on underneath.

ruched front

why: the folds deflect the eye from the flab.

low-waisted

why: waistband cuts across stomach making it half the size.

too tight, jean-cut

why: the stomach spills over the garrotting waistband.

worst trousers

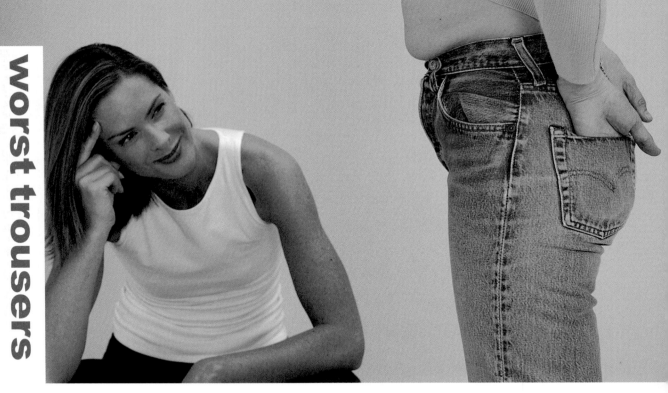

<u>or</u>

hipsters

why: too low to hide any stomach or leave a tummy with any dignity whatsoever.

flat-fronted with side zip

why: holds in tummy with no fuss at the front to bulk it up.

magic panties

why: these are the only suck-in pants that hoick up the arse and hold in the tummy without the squeezed excess spilling over the top like a frothing pint of Guinness. A must for every tummy carrier.

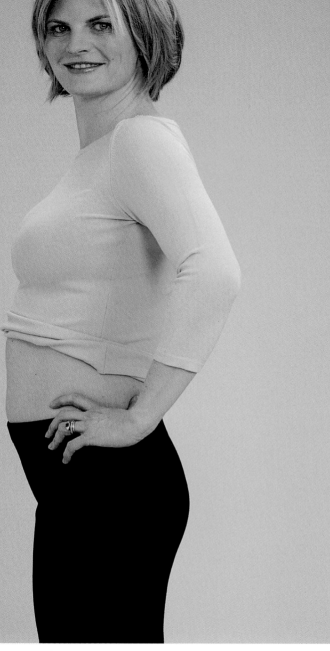

best trousers

alternative
low-waisted jeans one size too big

why: these hang loose around the waist making it look like the jeans are too big for your embarrassing secret.

belted

why: the belt creates gathers that increase the width of your uncontrollable girth.

worst coat

alternative
single-breasted buttoning from waist
why: left undone, this leaves only a sliver of the
underneath on show, which is very slimming.

best coat

**short-waisted
and fitted**
why: the tight waist
will encourage the
peplum to flare over
the tummy like a
little brim.

	no guilt	slight guilt	guilt for days
t-shirt	H & M Gap Target	Joseph BCBG Agnès b.	Helmut Lang Marni Chloé
top	H & M Chico's Banana Republic	Vanessa Bruno Katayone Adeli Catherine Malandrino	Tracy Feith Missoni
trousers	H & M Zara Gap	Joseph Nuala by Puma Paper Denim & Cloth	Calvin Klein Donna Karan
skirt	J. Crew H & M Club Monaco	Agnès b. Nanette Lepore	Jil Sander Rozae Nichols
jacket	H & M Zara Banana Republic	Joseph Dosa APC	Chloé Dolce & Gabbana Giorgio Armani

golden rules for flabby tummy

Never wear hipsters.

No skintight shiny fabrics.

Make sure clothes skim rather than cling.

Empire line dresses and tops hide the rolls.

Don't wear your belts too tight.

Make sure tops hang from tummy rather than go underneath it.

Don't be tempted to pierce a flabby belly button.

No cropped tops, even on baby fat.

golden rules

Style is wearing something no one else has

Excess fat at the side of the hips is an affliction common to millions of women. Like cellulite, it is **a burden carried by the female sex alone**. Unless a man is truly obese, he is saddlebag free. Saddlebags have the ability to make a skinny woman reach for the diet pills. The **"Does my ass look big in this?"** question will come into her head every time she gets dressed. "Yes, it does," comes our reply, "because you insist on wearing clothes that act as a neon sign to your expanding rear." If you are pear-shaped and carry your weight at the sides of your hips you'll doubtless find it hard to track down **decent-fitting trousers** and skirts that sit neatly on your waist and hips. You can then blame the size of your arse on the clothing industry, but isn't it better to be responsible for making the problem disappear?

saddlebags 8

big, white and baggy

why: even at the best of times these t-shirts...actually there are no best times with baggy t-shirts except when used as dusters...they turn a slightly distorted human being into one that has no waist as well as a pear-shaped bottom half.

slash neck

why: the width of the
neckline balances out the
width of those hips.

long wrap

why: wrap tops are a fabulous garment for reducing boobs and creating a waist, because the upper half of the top is nurturing these areas. In the case of saddlebags, it's the hem that has to do the work and sadly it's just not able to fit around stuffed hips. Try it yourself and you'll see the hem splays out at the widest part of your rear.

worst sweater

one that fits snugly and sits at the top of hips

why: clean, excess-fabric-free lines keep you slim atop, whilst a hem length that stops before the hips serves to reduce the waist to the extent that no one gives a toss about those bags.

alternative
cropped top

why: if you have saddlebags you will almost certainly have a narrower torso – hence the term pear-shaped. The best way of showing this off is to show a cheeky bit of tummy above not-too-tight hipsters.

tapered

why: we despise tapered trousers beyond all other garments. They should be outlawed from all corners of the globe and a maximum penalty should be given to those who wear them with saddlebags. If you have a pair, burn them, for the narrowness of the ankle only magnifies your hips by earth-shattering proportions.

or
straight leg

why: even these aren't wide enough at the hem to balance out your hips.

and
drainpipe jeans

why: these are the kiss of death for pear-shapes. All those rivets, pockets, belt loops and zips are too much for what's big and broad. This, coupled with skinny ankles, makes getting through the door a daily hazard.

flares

why: bring back the seventies and keep them there. Even if flares become unfashionable, saddlebag holders should hang on to them for dear life, for they are the only trousers that can reduce your bags to relative insignificance.

alternative
palazzo pants

why: the loose-fit fabric hangs from the bags erasing all knowledge of anything untoward going on underneath them.

best trousers

bias cut

why: the cross cut of the material makes it cling like a newborn on the breast to your hips. This is great for the hourglass, but style suicide for the pear-shape because it makes thunderous thighs positively torpedolike.

or
pencil shape

why: too tight for pear-shapes. Your saddlebags might as well be enlarged by the Hubble telescope and put on show at the Hayden Planetarium, so gross-making are these skirts for you.

A-line in any length

why: the material glides over and continues past the physical catastrophe, making it impossible for onlookers to become aware of your dark secret.

hacking jacket

why: any jacket that hits your hips at their widest part is terrible for you. You can get away with something shorter worn with an A-line skirt, but that proverbial hacking jacket length adds unnecessary stress to an already strained pair of hips.

or

funnel coat

why: if it fits around your butt, it won't fit anywhere else.

three-quarter length with flared hem

why: like an A-line skirt, the coat will wipe out the saddlebags.

best jacket

large lapels

why: a bold lapel balances out a broad beam by widening your chest and shoulders to keep up with the hips and create more of a waist.

	no guilt	slight guilt	guilt for days
top	H & M Petit Bateau Zara	Velvet Dosa	Marni Marc Jacobs
sweater	French Connection J. Crew Zara	Vanessa Bruno John Smedley DKNY	Marni Malo
trousers	Zara J. Crew	French Connection Jill Stuart BCBG	Calvin Klein Giorgio Armani Comme des Garçons
dress	Zara Club Monaco	APC Dosa Diane von Furstenburg	Marni Donna Karan
coat	Express Zara H & M	Theory French Connection Marc by Marc Jacobs	Prada Miu Miu Marc Jacobs Marni

golden rules for saddlebags

Never wear skirts or dresses cut on the bias – unless you want everyone to focus on your biggest defect.

Never wear jackets to the hip as you will only accentuate your thunder thighs.

Remember to balance out your shape by wearing A-line skirts and bootleg or flared trousers.

Coats are better than jackets.

Leggings are for the gym and nowhere else.

Put on an outfit you never end up wearing. Ask yourself exactly why it is not flattering.

Keep it all tidy – it will only work if you can find it

golden rules

You may think a short neck is of little or no importance. In fact, even if you have one you probably haven't noticed that your head grows straight from your shoulders. You are no doubt living in a long-necked paradise, bedecking yourself with all manner of **neck-throttling torture**. We can see you strangled by polo necks and hard for breath in a nonchalantly tied neckerchief. Handled badly, **a short neck can be aesthetically ruinous**. Look around you and pick out a chunky, clumping beast of a woman. She may be thin or fat, tall or short, but something about her makes her hulklike. Look closer and we bet you it's her **badly clad neck** that is turning her into our round-shouldered friend from Notre Dame. Short necks have the ability to **make the thin look fat**, the pretty ugly and when burdened by an extra chin or too, the young old before their years. Unfortunately, no lengthy starvation or deft handling of the scalpel is going to give the chinless a jaw or the neckless one worthy of a swan. This **can only be corrected by deception**.

turtleneck

why: as this poor man's polo neck travels halfway up the neck it leaves only the other half of what is an already pathetically short physical feature.

<u>or</u>
polo neck

why: if your lack of neck is also afflicted by an additional chin or two, they will hang over the top of the neck and you'll look like a turkey with a thyroid problem.

<u>and</u>
round neck

why: still too high for any kind of superficial elongation to have an effect.

9

alternative
wide scoop

why: reveals more of the shoulders, which, when pushed down by good posture, makes the neck longer and more elegant.

best neckline

deep V

why: opens up the whole chest area to create maximum exposure, which lengthens the neck.

Nehru

why: acts in exactly the same way as a turtleneck, which means aesthetic asphyxiation by a collar that looks too tight and over-powering for your impeded neck growth.

or.

collarless shirt

why: these are a mistake, especially for double chins. They do neither one thing nor the other and the loose flesh will overflow, making it the first thing you see appearing from the neckline.

turned-up
shirt collar

why: the height of the collar gives rise to a neck emerging gracefully from its folds. Be sure to button the shirt low to further elongate your neck.

best collar

9

a choker

why: will look more like a dog collar on a very dense bull terrier than a glamorous neck adornment. It's too overpowering for something so underdeveloped.

worst necklace

a fine choker

why: because of the delicate nature of the necklace, it gives your neck more room to shine on its own without being smothered.

no earrings

why: a short neck deprived of earrings is a short neck left wide open to scrutiny. Hanging down the side of it, earrings act as blinkers that blind the eye to the inadequate length of your gullet.

chandeliers

why: if the earring is long it will reflect its length on your neck. What happens is that the earrings carry the neck length up to your ear lobe as opposed to your jaw.

	no guilt	**slight guilt**	**guilt for days**
top	Gap Banana Republic J. Crew	APC Agnès b. Catherine Malandrino Vanessa Bruno	Chloé Gucci Stella McCartney
jewelry	Claire's H & M Express Girlshop.com	Anthropologie Agatha	Erickson Beamon Me & Ro
shirt	J. Crew Zara Club Monaco Gap	DKNY Calvin Klein Agnès b. French Connection	Comme des Garçons Paul Smith Jil Sander Dolce & Gabbana Calvin Klein Ralph Lauren

golden rules for short neck

The only time you can get away with a lot of gold is when it's in your mouth.

Short necks that hold a small head must never wear thick necklaces.

Long earrings are more flattering.

The longer the distance of flesh to the boobs – the longer the neck will look.

Turtlenecks will only enhance a squat neck.

Don't loop a pashmina – wrap it around twice.

The more flesh you show on your cleavage, the longer your neck will look.

Chuck out the clothes that don't suit you – even if you think of them as old friends.

Reassess your hairstyle.
Has it been the same for many years?
It may be safe but perhaps it's time
for a change

What makes a great Thoroughbred? Its ability to run like the wind thanks to fine-boned ankles. Thick ankles, by the same token, signify a more common breed in keeping with the Cob or Shire horse. Appreciated for their talent for pulling heavy goods and capacity to trudge through deeply ploughed furrows, their chunky fetlocks have long been revered by farmers and pit proprietors alike. Although we're not suggesting the only place a pair of **chunky human ankles** can get by is down the mine or knee-deep in manure, it would be fair to say that they **should be disguised whenever possible**. As should **a stout calf**, which can make even the skinniest women feel hefty and unfeminine. Summer is the worst enemy. While trousers are a great provider of camouflage and come in featherweight fabrics to keep you cool, you can't always be encased in slacks (and they provide an altogether different set of problems if they are the wrong shape). It's nice to **show a bit of leg** occasionally. So if you find a skirt length, and more importantly a shoe, to flatter your leg, then the heat can become your friend. The winter, of course, is heaps easier, as skirts of all lengths can be teamed with boots. But at the end of the day **the solution lies in becoming a master of illusion**. Do what David Copperfield does with airplanes and your ankles will disappear in a puff of smoke.

cropped to ankle

why: any trouser that ends mid-calf is a flying flag waving to a lower leg devoid of shape.

or
leggings

why: why bother wearing anything at all? Not only can we see the cellulite, but your criminal calves are going to get busted for blatantly flouting the law.

and
tapered jeans

why: there is a no more grotesque look than a calf getting caught up in the cling of jeans.

flared

why: no fabric can grip unbecomingly to the calf — instead, all is hidden and the leg is elongated when extra length hides a killer heel.

calf length

why: a thick calf in a medium-length skirt reminds us of an iceberg, only in this case it's the disproportionately large under-belly of it that's on display.

or
bias cut

why: a cross-cut fabric is born to cling seductively to the body. This means that anything appearing from below the hem will look huge by comparison.

and
ankle length

why: the only things poking out from underneath will be your pudgy ankles, making their very existence the sad focal point of your outfit.

A-line to the knee

why: the wider the skirt the slimmer the ankle and calf will appear.

ankle strap on the ankle

why: encircling the offending ankle will make it look like it's being throttled, thus drawing concerned attention to its welfare.

or
kitten-heel mule

why: the weight of the calf looks like it's not supported by the delicate heel and the closed toe chops the foot in half, thus visually depriving the leg of a good 3 or 4 inches.

and
pointed flat slip-on

why: the ankle is constricted by the delicacy of the shoe and appears even larger. These shoes also have a tendency to swell up the feet – making the ankle a total catastrophe.

open-toed, chunky-heeled sandal

why: the ankle is elongated right down to the toes, giving the appearance of a thinner leg.

alternative
wedge heel

why: the wedge is heavy enough to balance out the thickest of calves.

why: if you don't hold a pair of boots in your wardrobe, get out there now as they will make skirt wearing a joy.

or
calf-length boot

why: the meatiness of the calf will overflow. These are fine when the top of the boot is hidden.

and
ankle boots

why: this is a very dangerous form of footwear – it makes even the most refined legs look large and tarty. Fine under trousers, but put them on a thick calf and you'll see they are the worst accessory possible.

pull-on,
tight around the ankle

why: although difficult to locate, this shape that ends just under the knee is the best look. The calf is entirely covered up and they also work miracles on thick ankles. In fact, with these pull-ons, the bulkier the ankle the better.

best boots

alternative
high ankle boot

why: by hiding the ankle until the calf zone, the thickness is entirely hidden and well disguised.

	no guilt	slight guilt	guilt for days
skirt	H & M Zara J. Crew Anthropologie	Agnès b. Tocca French Connection APC Catherine Malandrino	Jil Sander Dries Van Noten Calvin Klein
trouser	Zara Miss Sixty Diesel H & M	French Connection DKNY 7 for all Mankind Joseph Plenty Theory	Chloé Plein Sud Marni Dolce & Gabbana Giorgio Armani Paul Smith
shoes	Zara Nine West Banana Republic Nina Steve Madden	Via Spiga Coach Charles David Sigerson Morrison	Dolce & Gabbana Christian Louboutin Prada Miu Miu Manolo Blahnik
boots	Zara Nine West J. Crew	Charles David Joseph Kenneth Cole	Walter Steiger Sergio Rossi Tod's Christian Louboutin Robert Clergerie

golden rules for thick ankles and calves

Kitten heels are unkind to thick ankles.

Never encircle the ankle – a strap should only be seen below.

Clingy skirts only emphasize the width above the foot.

Long skirts are made for thick ankles (even if you are under 5'2").

Boots are the savior for thick calves.

Never wear capri pants.

Never wear leggings except to the gym (and if you're single don't even go there).

Never wear three-quarter-length dresses or skirts.

golden rules

Black and brown shoes should never be worn with pale outfits

where to find it

7 for all Mankind
www.scoopnyc.com

A.B.S.
www.absstyle.com

Agatha
800-AGATHA7
www.agatha.fr.com

Agnès b.
www.agnesb.fr

Alberta Ferretti
www.albertaferretti.com

Alexander McQueen
www.alexandermcqueen.net

Alice + Olivia
www.aliceandolivia.com

Alice Temperley
www.temperleyxxii.com
www.net-a-porter.com

Anna Molinari
www.blumarine.com

Anthropologie
800-543-1039
www.anthropologie.com

Ballantyne
212-736-4228
www.ballantyne-cashmere.com

Banana Republic
888-BRSTYLE
www.bananarepublic.com

BCBG
888-636-BCBG
www.bcbg.com

Betsey Johnson
877-464-3293
www.betseyjohnson.com

Carmen Marc Valvo
888-4CARMEN
www.carmenmarcvalvo.com

Catherine Malandrino
www.catherinemalandrino.com

Charles David
310-348-5041
www.charlesdavid.com

Chloé
www.chloe.com

Christian Louboutin
www.christian-louboutin.silkrunway.com

Claire's
1600 stores
www.claires.com

Club Monaco
www.clubmonaco.com

Coach
www.coach.com

Comme des Garçons
www.comme-des-garcons.silkrunway.com

Costume National
www.costumenational.com

Cynthia Rowley
www.cynthiarowley.com

Diane von Furstenberg
www.dvf.com

Diesel
212-755-9200
www.diesel.com

DKNY
www.dkny.com

Dolce & Gabbana
www.dolcegabbana.it

Donna Karan
www.donnakaran.com

Dosa
mail@dosainc.com

Dries van Noten
www.driesvannoten.be

Earl Jean
www.earljean.com

Erickson Beaman
www.net-a-porter.com

Etro
www.etro.it

Express
www.expressfashion.com

French Connection
www.frenchconnection.com

GAP
800-GAP-STYLE
www.gap.com

Ghost
www.ghost.co.uk

Georgina Von Etzdorf
www.gve.co.uk

Giorgio Armani
www.giorgioarmani.com

Girlshop.com
www.girlshop.com

Gucci
www.gucci.com

H & M
www.hm.com

Helmut Lang
www.helmutlang.com

J. Crew
800-932-0043
www.jcrew.com

Jil Sander
www.jilsander.com

Jill Stuart
www.jillstuart.com

John Galliano
www.johngalliano.com

John Smedley
www.johnsmedley.com

Joseph
212-343-7071

Juicy Couture
www.juicycouture.com
www.shopbop.com

Katayone Adeli
www.net-a-porter.com

Kate Spade
www.katespade.com

Kenneth Cole
800-KEN-COLE
www.kennethcole.com

Laundry
www.edressme.com/laundry.html

Malo
www.itholding.it
www.designerexposure.com

Marc Jacobs
www.marcjacobs.com
www.eluxury.com

Marc by Marc Jacobs
www.marcjacobs.com
www.eluxury.com

Marni
www.net-a-porter.com

MaxMara
www.milanfashionshows.com/
spring2003/maxmara/photos.htm

Michael Kors
www.michaelkors.com

directory

Missoni

www.missoni.com

Miss Sixty

www.misssixty.com
www.shopbop.com

Miu Miu

www.miumiu.com

Nanette Lepore

www.nanettelepore.com

Nicole Farhi

www.nicolefarhi.com

Nina

www.ninashoes.com
www.nordstromshoes.com

Nine West

www.ninewest.com

Nuala

888-565-7862
www.nuala.puma.com

Old Navy

800-OLD-NAVY
www.oldnavy.com

Paper Denim & Cloth

www.scoopnyc.com

Paul & Joe

www.net-a-porter.com

Paul Smith

www.net-a-porter.com

Petit Bateau

212-988-8884
www.petit-bateau.com

Plein Sud

212-431-6500

Plenty

www.getplenty.com

Prada

www.prada.com

Pucci

www.emiliopucci.com

Roland Mouret

www.net-a-porter.com

Rozae Nichols

212-944-7900
www.neimanmarcus.com

Sergio Rossi

www.sergiorossi.com

Sigerson Morrison

www.sigersonmorrison.com

Stella McCartney

www.stellamccartney.com

Steve Madden

www.stevemadden.com

Target

www.target.com

directory

Theory
www.theory.com
www.shopbop.com

Thomas Pink
888-336-1192
www.thomaspink.com

Three Dots
www.frenchkids.com

Tocca
www.tocca.com

Tod's
www.tods.com

Tommy Hilfiger
www.tommy.com

Tracy Feith
www.tracyfeith.com

TSE cashmere
Corporate Headquarters
3001 S. Croddy Way
Santa Ana, CA 92704
714-957-4000

Tuleh
www.designerexposure.com

Vanessa Bruno
www.net-a-porter.com

Velvet
www.shopbop.com

Veronique Branquinho
www.barneys.com

Versace
www.versace.com

Via Spiga
www.nordstromshoes.com

Vivienne Westwood
www.viviennewestwood.com

Yves St. Laurent
www.ysl.com

Zara
www.zara.com

major department stores

Barneys

6 stores in the U.S.
Madison Avenue at 61st Street
New York, NY
212-826-8900
www.barneys.com

Bergdorf Goodman

Fifth Avenue at 58th Street
New York, NY
212-753-7300

Bloomingdales

29 stores in the U.S.
Lexington Avenue at 59th Street
New York, NY
212-705-2000
www.bloomingdales.com

Fred Segal's

West Hollywood
8118 Melrose Avenue
323-651-4129 (Ron Herman)

Henri Bendel

712 Fifth Avenue
New York, NY
800-HBENDEL

Macy's

200 stores in the U.S.
151 W. 34th Street
New York, NY
212-695-4400
www.macys.com

Neiman Marcus

30 stores in the U.S.
888-888-4757
www.neimanmarcus.com

Nordstrom

143 stores in the U.S.
888-282-6060
www.nordstrom.com

Parisian

42 stores in the U.S.
Phipps Plaza Mall
3500 Peachtree Rd NE
Atlanta, GA
404-814-3200
www.parisian.com

Saks Fifth Avenue

60 stores in the U.S.
Fifth Avenue at 49th Street
New York, NY
877-551-SAKS
www.saks.com

directory

designers' own label stores by city

Aspen

Malo

520 East Durant
970-925-3111

Prada

Andres Building
312 South Galena Street
970-925-7001

Tod's

200 South Mill Street
970-925-7575

Atlanta

MaxMara

Phipps Plaza Mall
3500 Peachtree Road NE
404-814-6095

Versace

Phipps Plaza Mall
3500 Peachtree Road
404-814-0664

Boston

Giorgio Armani

22 Newbury Street
617-267-3200

Kate Spade

117 Newbury Street
617-262-2632

Chicago

Cynthia Rowley

808 West Armitage Avenue
773-528-6160

Giorgio Armani

800 North Michigan Avenue
312-751-2244

Jil Sander
48 East Oak Street
312-335-0006

Kate Spade
101 East Oak Street
312-654-8853

Malo
909 North Michigan Avenue
312-440-1060

MaxMara
900 North Michigan Avenue
312-475-9500

Prada
30 East Oak Street
312-951-1113

Ralph Lauren
One Magnificent Mile
750 North Michigan Avenue
312-280-1655

Tod's
121 East Oak Street
312-943-0070

Dallas

Calvin Klein
444 Highland Park
214-520-9222

MaxMara
Dallas Galleria
13355 Noel Road
972-386-6078

Versace
13350 Dallas Parkway, Suite 1495
972-385-9155

Houston

MaxMara
Houston Galleria
5015 Westheimer Road
713-626-5617

Versace
Houston Galleria
5015 Westheimer Road, Suite 2340
713-623-8220

Yves St. Laurent
Houston Galleria
5015 Westheimer Road
713-840-7006

Las Vegas

Dolce & Gabbana
Caesar's Palace
3500 Las Vegas Boulevard South, Suite B7
702-892-0880

Giorgio Armani
Bellagio—The Resort
3600 Las Vegas Boulevard South
702-893-8347

MaxMara
Caesar's Palace
3500 Las Vegas Boulevard South
702-732-0900

Prada
Bellagio—The Resort
3600 Las Vegas Boulevard South #22
702-866-6886

Tod's
Caesar's Palace
3500 Las Vegas Boulevard South
702-792-1422

Versace
Caesar's Palace
3500 Las Vegas Boulevard South
702-796-7222

Yves St. Laurent
Bellagio—The Resort
3600 Las Vegas Boulevard South
702-737-3003

Los Angeles
Catherine Malandrino
8644 Sunset Boulevard
310-360-1037

Christian Louboutin
9040 Burton Way
310-247-9300

Costume National
8001 Melrose Avenue
323-655-8160

Cynthia Rowley
7975 Melrose Avenue
323-658-7642

Dolce & Gabbana
312 North Rodeo Drive
301-888-8701

Ghost
125 North Robertson Boulevard
310-246-0567

Giorgio Armani
436 North Rodeo Drive
310-271-5555

MaxMara
323 North Rodeo Drive
310-385-9343

Prada
469 North Rodeo Drive
310-385-5959

Sergio Rossi
366 North Rodeo Drive
310-271-9333

Sigerson Morrison
8307 West 3rd Street
310-655-6133

Tod's
333 North Rodeo Drive
310-285-0591

Versace
248 North Rodeo Drive
310-205-3921

Miami
Diane von Furstenberg
The Village at Merrick Park
320 San Lorenzo Avenue
305-446-4003

Dolce & Gabbana
9700 Collins Avenue, Unit 151
305-866-0503

directory

d

Etro

The Village at Merrick Park
342 San Lorenzo Avenue
305-569-1669

Giorgio Armani

9700 Collins Avenue
305-861-1515

Malo

9700 Collins Avenue
305-861-0600

MaxMara

9700 Collins Avenue
305-867-2210

Me & Ro

1901 Collins Avenue
305-672-3566

Prada

9700 Collins Avenue
305-864-9111

Sergio Rossi

9700 Collins Avenue
305-868-1658

Tod's

9700 Collins Avenue
305-867-9399

Versace

9700 Collins Avenue
305-864-0044

Yves St. Laurent

9700 Collins Avenue
305-868-4424

New York, NY

Alberta Ferretti

452 Broadway
212-632-9336

Alexander McQueen

417 W. 14th Street
212-645-1797

Calvin Klein

654 Madison Avenue
212-292-9000

Catherine Malandrino

468 Broome Street
212-925-6765

Chloé

850 Madison Avenue
212-717-8220

Christian Louboutin

941 Madison Avenue
212-396-1884

Coach

595 Madison Avenue
212-754-0041

Comme des Garçons

520 W. 22nd Street
212-604-9200

Costume National

108 Wooster Street
212-431-1530

Cynthia Rowley

112 Wooster Street
212-334-1144

directory

Diane von Furstenberg
385 W. 12th Street
646-486-4800

Dolce & Gabbana
825 Madison Avenue
212-249-4100

Donna Karan
819 Madison Avenue
212-861-1001

Dosa
107 Thompson Street
212-431-1733

Erickson Beamon
498 7th Avenue, Suite 2404
212-643-4810

Etro
720 Madison Avenue
212-317-9096

Ghost
28 Bond Street
646-602-2891

Giorgio Armani
760 Madison Avenue
212-988-9191

Gucci
685 Fifth Avenue
212-826-2600

Helmut Lang
80 Greene Street
212-334-1014

Jil Sander
11 E. 57th Street
212-838-6100

Jill Stuart
100 Greene Street
212-343-2300

Katayone Adeli
35 Bond Street
212-260-3500

Kate Spade
454 Broome Street
212-274-1991

Kors by Michael Kors
159 Mercer Street
212-966-5880

Malo
814 Madison Avenue
212-396-4721

Marc Jacobs
163 Mercer Street
212-343-1490

Marc by Marc Jacobs
403 Bleecker Street
212-924-0026

MaxMara
813 Madison Avenue
212-879-6100

Me & Ro
239 Elizabeth Street
917-237-9215

Michael Kors
974 Madison Avenue
212-452-4685

Missoni
1009 Madison Avenue
212-517-9339

Miu Miu
100 Prince Street
212-334-5156

Nanette Lepore
423 Broome Street
212-219-8265

Nicole Farhi
10 E. 60th Street
212-223-8811

Paul & Joe
2 Bond Street
212-505-0974

Paul Smith
108 Fifth Avenue
212-627-9770

Prada
45 E. 57th Street
212-308-2332

Pucci
24 E. 64th Street
212-752-4777

Ralph Lauren
867 Madison Avenue
212-606-2100
381 West Broadway
212-625-1660

Sergio Rossi
772 Madison Avenue
212-327-4288

Sigerson Morrison
28 Prince Street
212-219-3893

Stella McCartney
429 W. 14th Street
212-255-1556

Tod's
650 Madison Avenue
212-644-5945

Tracy Feith
209 Mulberry Street
212-334-3097

TSE
827 Madison Avenue
212-472-7790

Tuleh
181 Chrystie Street
212-979-7888

Versace
815 Madison Avenue
212-744-5572

Yves St. Laurent
855 Madison Avenue
212-988-3821

Palm Beach
Giorgio Armani
243 Worth Avenue
561-655-1641

directory

Malo

228 Worth Avenue
561-655-3312

MaxMara

216 Worth Avenue
561-832-0069

Pucci

Esplanade 150 Worth Avenue
561-655-7070

Ralph Lauren

300 Worth Avenue
561-651-3900

San Francisco

Giorgio Armani

278 Post Street
415-434-2500

Kate Spade

227 Grant Avenue
415-216-0880

Marc Jacobs

125 Maiden Lane
415-362-6500

MaxMara

175 Post Street
415-981-0900

Prada

140 Geary Street
415-391-8844

TSE cashmere

60 Maiden Lane
415-391-1112

Versace

60 Post Street
415-616-0604

Yves St. Laurent

166 Maiden Lane
415-837-1211

Washington, D.C.

Relish

5454 Wisconsin Avenue
Chevy Chase, MD
301-654-9899

Saks Jandel

5510 Wisconsin Avenue
Chevy Chase, MD
301-652-2250

directory